Envisioning Peace
Educating Through Narratives:
Understanding Our Stories to Learn and Teach

ENVISIONING PEACE
EDUCATING THROUGH NARRATIVES:
UNDERSTANDING OUR STORIES TO LEARN AND TEACH

Susan Francis Carson

WHAT OTHERS ARE SAYING . . .

"In *Envisioning Peace*, Susan Carson shows how teachers can use the stories of children in their classrooms to counter the prevailing 'deficit' models of education that are currently dominant. But she never makes it a 'lesson,' instead offering the stories as a choice. By truly being present in the lives of all children, teachers have the power to alter students' lives toward more freedom, happiness, and peace. Listening with empathy and caring for students ultimately promotes well-being and, as a result, greater learning.

I predict that you will walk away from this book with new insights into the powerful forces that seem to predetermine our lives and how self-compassion and compassion for others may counter these forces. Susan Carson has created a big-hearted manual on an often overlooked, but critical topic. Brava!"

Elaine Collins, Ph.D.
President, Johnson State College
Former Dean, College of Education
Grand Valley State University

"Susan Carson offers narratives that illustrate how people grappled with conflict and pursued processes for the advancement of peace. This book is a curriculum asset in schools that have committed to the development of compassion and caring. Teacher preparation programs will be enhanced with the guidance it offers, and this is an important resource for study circles and counseling."

Candice C. Carter, Ph.D.
Associate Dean, College of Education and Counseling Psychology
Saint Martin's University

"This book is wonderful and very deep and wide! Through sharing our stories/experiences we receive Wisdom. From Wisdom, Love and Compassion arise. Our lives are naturally transformed into an expression of service to others. Susan Carson's book is an offering of Loving Wisdom with the power to open our hearts to Life."

Krishna Das
Chant Master and Grammy Award Nominee

"This is a spiritual book because it combines individuality and commonality. Susan Carson has shown us, in touching ways, how peace in the world links to our personal story."

David Richo, Ph.D., M.F.T.
Psychotherapist, Teacher, Workshop Leader, and Writer

"*Envisioning Peace* is a book written by an educator for educators. But it's clear from the beginning that Carson is working from Maya Angelou's framework that we are all teachers, 'whether we know it or not, whether we take responsibility for it or not.' This book is a lesson in the power of acceptance and love. It is an easy thing to quote scripture, an easy thing to think about the struggles Carson talks about as ideas. It's much harder to actually live the concepts of love, hope, forgiveness, openness to difference. The people in her stories show us the way."

Cecilia Skidmore, M.A., L.P.C.
Co-founder and Therapist, Third Coast Counseling

DEDICATION

I want to thank the individuals who shared their stories with me. Their narratives are only partially explored in this book. However, these stories can serve as guides for the ultimate responsibilities of educators and the potentially transformative power of caring in education. These individuals are champions in their own lives. They have battled adversity and surfaced as testimonies to the power of individuals caring for one another.

ACKNOWLEDGMENTS

THIS WORK IS THE RESULT of loving care and support from numerous individuals. *Envisioning Peace* has been an ongoing pursuit for myself and many others.

To all of my teachers and to my students who continue to teach me how to be my best self, thank you. My deepest gratitude goes to my family for being by my side, living and learning. And without my editor's gentle guidance, the depth of meaning of my words would have been lost.

Finally, a heartfelt appreciation to my partner who has steadfastly joined in life with me.

Envisioning Peace

TABLE OF CONTENTS

What Others Are Saying v

Dedication · vii

Acknowledgments ·ix

Introduction · xiii

Chapter 1 The Path · 1

Chapter 2 Cindy & Dorie: The Power of Family · · · · · · · · · · · · · · · · · 7

Chapter 3 Journee: Spiritual Quest & Practice · · · · · · · · · · · · · · · 19

Chapter 4 John: In Our Schools · 27

Chapter 5 Hannah: A Struggle for Well-Being · · · · · · · · · · · · · 37

Chapter 6 Isaiah: The Courage to Begin Again · · · · · · · · · · · · · · · · 47

Chapter 7 On the Streets · 57

Simple Guide · 69

References & Resources · 71

About the Author · 77

INTRODUCTION

ENVISIONING PEACE IS A COLLECTION of individual narratives and commentaries meant for everyone, but especially educators.

Maya Angelou discussed what it means to become who we were meant to be. "... I am a teacher. I teach all the time ... as all of you do — whether we know it or not, whether we take responsibility for it or not."

The hidden curriculum of teaching lies in opportunities to learn. True learning comes when we connect with and teach each other, whatever our life's work is.

One of my fundamental truths in teaching is "know yourself, know your students." In the fast-paced profession of education we need to take the time to acknowledge our own story and get to know our students' stories. When that happens trust is built, connections occur, and the power of compassion and care in education come to the forefront.

The struggle in learning can be shared. Peace can be generated by understanding who we are and sharing our stories. We do not stand alone. The narratives in this book demonstrate this. They are glimpses into the lives of people like you and me.

As you read each narrative, envision how, as an educator, you could connect with these brave people. How can our practices be enhanced by understanding different family structures? Do we leave out students who are adopted, fostered, or looking for a home? How ignored is mental health in educating the minds of our students? Do we recognize the importance of different spiritual practices and religions in our classes?

How are behavior challenges addressed? Are we unknowingly abandoning students to the streets?

These stories address some of life's major challenges and show how these individuals have transformed their lives through the power of compassion and care, illuminating both our profound diversity and our connectedness. Life narratives like these convince me that caring for others and envisioning a peaceful means to live can unite all of us — if we're willing to listen and understand.

Ultimately, the narratives in *Envisioning Peace* are examples of how sharing stories can be a tool for promoting the possibility for change. They implore us to go beyond ourselves, to jump into the transformative nature of storytelling, to become one with the storyteller and the story, and to learn and grow as individuals and residents of this wonderful world.

CHAPTER 1

THE PATH

"People take different roads seeking fulfillment and happiness.
Just because they're not on your road doesn't mean
they've gotten lost."
- His Holiness the 14th Dalai Lama, Tenzin Gyatso

Envisioning Peace

Storytelling

STORYTELLING IS AN ANCIENT ART that we still celebrate and practice today. We are who we are partly because of the stories we hear as we grow up. The legends of our ancestry — when told with a rich sense of adventure, adversity, failure, and success — hold vast promise to entertain, educate, pass on our culture, and instill a sense of moral values.

Truly listening to others' stories creates opportunities to resonate with them and to shape awareness and consciousness in our own lives. We have the potential to change our attitudes, become kinder, and learn how to be more compassionate when we understand others' stories.

Teaching

Education, too, is an ancient art that began with the spoken word well before the introduction of written language (3500 B.C.E.). Oral storytelling traditions have enabled us to pass knowledge and wisdom down throughout generations and cultures. In teaching, as in telling stories, our words carry many meanings. They can confuse and belittle, or they can instruct, inspire, and heal. We build relationships with our language and actions, for good or for ill, when we teach.

The challenge of creating and maintaining positive, peaceful, caring practices in our work often appears unattainable — an insurmountable problem of assimilation. The hustle and bustle of an educator's life demands considerable acumen — a balancing act of priorities in a measured amount of time. The responsibility for teaching with care rests with the individual. Being responsible in this way empowers one's self as well as others. So conditions need to be created where the individual pursuit of care in education is reinforced by the support of others. Within this individual expression lie threads that bind us all in our collective humanity and desire to be cared for.

Personal Narratives

How often have we been told to pay attention? Yet actively listening and being aware of ourselves often falls between the cracks of busyness. Life passes fast. We must learn to be present in our own lives; this is especially true for teachers, who carry so much responsibility for others.

One way to be "here" is to be conscious of our personal narratives. Our stories give us insights into who we are and what we cherish. They give us mental and emotional sustenance, helping us to be more comfortable in our own identity.

Our personal stories also create a framework that helps us share ourselves with the world and the people we have relationships with. Effective relationships are integral to our success as individuals, mothers, fathers, sisters, brothers, friends, colleagues, and everyday acquaintances. And these relationships combine to create our communities — local, regional, and global.

Community

The importance of community can be traced back through ancient civilizations. An ideal community, according to Gandhi and Socrates, is one that resembles the human body. The individual parts, each designed to complete a specific function, must work together for the whole to function.

Gandhi stated that communities, despite all their complexity, must function in synchronicity. This is imperative to avoid destruction and violence. The care and peace that we want to experience as individuals must happen for all. This concept of "all" includes particularly the vulnerable populations related to (but certainly not limited to) gender, culture, race, sexual orientation, and socioeconomic position.

Our individual stories have the potential to generate this synchronicity and bring us together in community. Sharing individual stories tends to create bonds of understanding and empathy with others, multiplying the possibilities for learning and change. Because hearing others' narratives influences our attitudes and consciousness, we can transform not only ourselves but our communities through the power of storytelling.

GLOBAL CONNECTIONS

In addition to personal and community transformation, stories can be used to bring our world together. They are powerful gifts for international communication. They can be used to solve problems, create goodwill, and uplift humanity.

Personal narratives often reflect community and global concerns. Within the personal lies the universal. No matter where we live or how diverse we are, we all need to care and be cared for. And we all want our individual narratives to be heard and respected.

To achieve caring, connection, and peace at the global level is hard work. There is only one place to start — with our own lives and our own stories. We are the agents of change in our lives. Every day that we affirm the inherent dignity of everyone . . . help to maintain a climate of justice marked by respect, integrity, and caring for each other . . . foster mutual understanding . . . confirm freedom of expression with civility and decency . . . and express individuality within bounds of courtesy, sensitivity, and respect, we are living what the Dalai Lama believes — that all human beings are brothers and sisters.

THE NARRATIVE BLANKET

The five narratives in this book are examples of how listening to our students' stories can increase our collective capacity to envision the peace that is so needed in our lives and in the world. They can empower educators to gain a greater understanding of the lives our students live, the stories they are telling.

There are distinct threads woven throughout these narratives, ultimately creating a blanket that supports our work in the world. Family is one thread, meaning the community we belong to that enriches and nurtures our lives. Spirituality is another strand. Whether we practice a religion or not, we're all deeply spiritual people governed by our values. Teaching and learning can also be found in this blanket.

Hopes and challenges are among the other threads that make up the blanket we are weaving. What are our hopes? How do we handle our challenges? Do we even acknowledge that we can dream, that we can envision our lives and bring those dreams into reality?

Finally, how do we put it all together? How do we utilize the foundation of the work we have done? How do we use this blanket we have woven? How can we be "here" as we teach and actively engage in our daily business, both routine and profound?

CHAPTER 2

CINDY & DORIE:
THE POWER OF FAMILY

"Oh, the comfort, the inexpressible comfort of feeling safe
with a person;
having neither to weigh thoughts nor measure words,
but pouring them all right out, just as they are,
chaff and grain together,
certain that a faithful hand will take and sift them,
keep what is worth keeping,
and then, with the breath of kindness, blow the rest away."
- Dinah Craik

Envisioning Peace

THESE WORDS FROM CINDY AND Dorie's wedding announcement echoed in my mind as I pulled up to their home, sorting through my car in temperatures hovering from 10-20 below, searching for my "regular" glasses. I often misplaced them, but now I was in their driveway, with Dorie waiting at the door, dogs barking. Oh well, I could always take my sunglasses off and squint.

Family could be found here — that amazing comfort that comes from being okay, being who I am (glasses or not). I was welcomed with a question from Dorie. "Do you know where this antique serving dish comes from? It comes from my ex-husband's current wife, Connie. She came over with her son for Christmas Eve. We played games and had a great Christmas Eve."

Dorie was born in Grand Rapids, Michigan, on February 20, 1931. She creates ease with her communication style.

"Do you want to sit at the table?" Cindy asked, as we moved into their home. Cindy was also born in Grand Rapids — on October 10, 1949. "Let's be comfortable; where do you want to sit?"

I asked if they had a favorite place. "We sit together on this." Cindy indicated a reclining loveseat. "We have had this rebuilt because we cannot find another that fits us so well." So began their narrative of 46 years of partnership.

Cindy remarked, "When we went into our relationship I don't remember any thoughts about short-term anything. If we are going to do this, we are going to do this."

"I always knew I was gay, but I can't remember what word we used back then," Dorie commented.

Dorie originally went into nursing and she had a "thing" with her roommate. But her roommate ended up getting pregnant and told Dorie, "This will never work; we could never be together."

"So I said phooey to this," Dorie explained. "I decided I guess I will go along with everybody else." She married and had four children.

"As the years went by, I knew there was something missing. I was miserable. At this point I met Cindy at the nursing home where I worked; she was just a student working weekends as an aide."

Dorie waited a few moments and then added, "I don't know that we have talked about it many times. I don't know why, with 18 years difference in age, but we immediately just liked everything together."

Cindy smiled. "I knew I was different from a very young age. I didn't do the prom thing. I had my little group of girlfriends that I did everything with. Boys and men weren't included. But it was still kinda that time of life, being in school and with my friends dating. So I dated this guy from church. He was older than I was, and he went to school at Michigan Tech. My parents thought this was really a good deal, so I would go up and spend the weekends with him and come back.

"When Dorie and I first started talking at the nursing home, she was miserable and I was miserable. Then people there picked up that there was something more than just friends about our relationship."

The ensuing family struggle to accept, understand, and move on took time — complete with a divorce for Dorie, legal threats over public displays of affection like holding hands, hard words, and rebellious children. Cindy and Dorie worked through it all, opening their home for family and friends who needed a place to stay or help recovering from surgeries or cancer treatments.

They took care of Dorie's brother when he got out of prison with cancer, and set him up in his own home. When he died, they transformed his home into a transitional home for ex-prisoners. They casually refer to themselves as "do-gooders," and their work continues.

As in a lot of caring work, there is often a tendency to leave oneself out. Dorie observed, "When I was sick once Cindy said, 'I don't know how to put gas in the car.' I thought, 'Geeze I've got to get better.'"

As we finished talking in their home that chilly day, Dorie emphasized how important their friendships are. "We have met some wonderful people. We are so damn lucky."

Cindy quickly added, "Every morning we have a gratitude thing we do. We *are* lucky."

Human Families

Those that we are born to, nurtured by, and develop relationships with create our first experience of family. The diversity of our families contributes to the creation of our unique personalities. Within this family of origin we begin to build the foundation of our lives — the people we gravitate toward, the educational opportunities we have, and the experiences we gather. Our personal narratives begin.

Families come in all sizes and types. A family can be found in a tribe, a nuclear or single-parent household, a stepfamily, a reconstituted family, even in kinship with friends. Many cultures have extended families that include relatives, particularly grandparents or elders. Some families are gay; some are straight. Some have children — biological, adopted, fostered, or nurtured through contact with teachers or community advocates. Ultimately, as we grow up we end up defining our own family.

Stories From Our Families

There is a Buddhist apothegm that states before we are conceived we pick our parents and the environment we will be born into. From that perspective, it's important that we learn lessons from our parents and the circumstances that arise from growing up in that particular environment.

Our experiences as children can create powerful lifelong bonds with others in our family of origin or create challenges that separate us permanently. Regardless of what happens, everything can be used as an opportunity to learn something — even damaging words and actions that haven't been healed or forgiven.

Family stories can often be a path to growth and healing when we are willing to be brave, to drop our defenses, and truly hear another's story. Our family members carry unique knowledge about who we are because they laid down the psychological and physical framework we grew up in. If we're willing to listen to them, we can begin to understand ourselves from a deep place where patterns and habits began.

"Family" in Communities

Humans are a social species with a need to belong and bond with others beyond our families of origin. Although this sense of belonging is most deeply rooted in whatever relationships we understand to be family, the feeling of "family" can be found in communities.

There are geographical communities; our neighbors and the neighborhoods we live in can play a large role in delineating who we call family. There also are activity-based communities, religious-based communities, political communities, school communities, and work communities. The possibilities for finding family connections within communities are numerous. But always, it is within these bonds that our individual stories are shaped and shared.

FAMILIES BEYOND FAMILY

Life's experiences can bring us into contact with others who recognize us at some level we might not fully understand. We know immediately that they are part of "our tribe," even if we cannot say why.

When souls are brought together like this, they help us do life's work; they lift us up on our path, unite us, and help us recognize our wholeness. When this happens, our concept of family grows beyond the biological or community level. Deep connections are made, and the threads of our stories come together in the wonderful interlacing of the warp and weft of our lives.

This can occur on a worldwide scale. In a 2014 commencement speech at the University of Texas at Austin, Admiral William McRaven began by stating that the average American will meet 10,000 people in their lifetime. He challenged the graduating class of approximately 8,000 students to change the lives of 10 people for the better. If each of those 10 individuals changed the lives of another 10 people, in five generations (125 years) they would have changed the lives of 800 million people — more than twice the current population of the United States. In six generations the entire population of the world would be touched.

This is family on a grand scale — the human family working together to envision peace and well-being for everyone. When hearts touch hearts, and stories are passed from one generation to another, possibilities for change and hope are created.

OUR CLASSROOMS AS FAMILY

Students in the United States are in school 175-180 days each year, with approximately 900-1,000 hours of instruction time, depending on state requirements. It is estimated that teachers spend more time with their students than some students spend with their families. Teachers have many responsibilities and roles throughout their day: educator, counselor, nurse, and surrogate parent. There are typically one instructor and 30 students per classroom.

I'm fond of saying that it is "our" class and not "my" class. Creating communities of learners is fundamental in effective teaching. Building classroom families/communities with an understanding of the rights and responsibilities of the learners requires a strong foundation of respect, collaboration, and trust. Neurological research has shown that students learn best when they feel safe and have low stress levels. When students can support each other in learning, they can take risks and challenge each other, knowing that they'll be supported if they don't succeed first time out. This culture of learning enables students to feel they belong, promoting a sense of competency and the desire to learn.

Belonging in a classroom family can bring us to a destiny in our lives, where we get the occasion to carry on the process of lifelong learning, advancing the knowledge of ourselves and the world we live in. Learning is then wherever we look, wherever we go, and in all of our interactions with one another.

LGBTQQ STUDENTS IN THE CLASSROOM

For educators, creating a sense of family and belonging in the classroom means *all* students need to be accepted, cared for, feel safe to be themselves, and comfortable in their own identity. This is part of our daily work.

In one of my classes there was a student who became more and more agitated as parent-teacher conferences grew near. At the very mention, she would squirm in her desk and then approach me later saying that her parents were coming. I would tell her I was looking forward to meeting them. This pattern happened several times. She was an excellent student and didn't have any academic concerns. She was well liked and got along with everyone. When the conferences occurred her parents introduced themselves to me; they were a lesbian couple. I got it. I finally understood her reluctance. She didn't know how I would react.

The statistics on LGBTQQ (Lesbian, Gay, Bisexual, Transgender, Queer, Questioning) individuals and societal acceptance are changing. Currently there are 36 states, the District of Columbia, and 21 Native American tribal jurisdictions that recognize same-sex marriage. More than 70% of Americans live in areas where same-sex couples can marry. The 2010 census report showed that approximately six million American children and adults have an LGBT parent.

But still, the challenges of raising children and interacting with schools and teachers often become compounded with same-sex parents. Court decisions supporting gay marriage are often overshadowed by debates over whether school counselors can opt out of working with LGBTQQ youth due to a potential conflict with religious beliefs. It is estimated that 3-5% of youth in the United States are lesbian, gay, bisexual, or transgender. The Gay, Lesbian and Straight Education Network (GLSEN) 2014 National School Climate Survey stated that 74% of LGBT youth are subjected to verbal harassment at school. The Forty to None Project estimated that 20-40% of all homeless youth in the United States are lesbian, gay, bisexual, or transgender. And LGBTQQ youth have an exponentially higher suicide rate — eight times that of their heterosexual peers.

We can't waste so much talent. As an educator, you need to be prepared to teach everyone. Know your students. Understand their backgrounds and families. If you don't understand, take steps to gain another perspective. Talk with religious leaders who support LGBTQQ individuals and attend conferences designed for acceptance of LGBT students. Expand your perspective. Be open to learn. Envision peace along the way.

Cindy and Dorie Revisited

Cindy and Dorie have created a loving family that continues to grow and flourish daily beyond their 46-year history together, even though the journey has not been easy for them. Both professionally and personally, they have mastered the art of caring for each other against all odds while also caring for others in their own backyard.

Dorie recently grappled with cellulitis complications. She emerged out of a multiple-day hospital stay exhausted and still battling the infection. But by working with doctors, trying different medications, and being cared for by Cindy, she regained her health.

While this was going on, their lives did not stop. A friend of Dorie's brother, Emilio, was released from prison. Cindy and Dorie opened their home and hearts to him. Emilio joined with them at their church and became part of their family.

When I last visited with Cindy and Dorie, they were trying to figure out how to deliver a car they had purchased for Emilio. The car didn't have proper registration papers or a license plate. (He was going to register the car as soon as he passed the driver's test.) They needed to drive the car to where Emilio now lived. Dorie joked, "The police officer will see an old lady driving and not bother to pull me over or give me a ticket." Well, Dorie was pulled over. But she wasn't ticketed, and the police officer escorted her to her final destination.

This is just one of many small stories. In their daily lives, Cindy and Dorie show what is possible in a world free from hatred, fear, and intolerance — where everyone is accepted, cared for, safe to be themselves, and comfortable in their own identity.

CHAPTER 3

JOURNEE: SPIRITUAL QUEST & PRACTICE

All the world is our home, we are all family.
- Tvameva Mata from Vedas Scriptures

Journee told me that her story began June 29, 1954, when she was baptized in Mishawaka, Indiana, surrounded by family and godparents. Her early memories of church were of special occasions, such as Easter and Christmas. Learning focused on being quiet, going to Sunday school, the Bible, and Jesus.

Journee was confirmed at age 12 in St. Michael's Church Episcopal in Racine, Wisconsin. "Church took on a new dimension and became an active part of my life," she explained. "The youth group led by a young priest and his wife began to have deeper meaning. I knew that there was a higher power outside and within myself. 'Peace be with you' had great meaning for me."

Eventually, Journee went to college in Boulder, Colorado, in the 1970s, majoring in molecular, cellular, and developmental biology. She loved the precision of math and science, but something was missing.

One summer, Boulder exploded into a spiritual Mecca. Chögyam Trungpa came to town, followed by Allan Ginsberg, William Burroughs, and other seekers. Oscar Ichazo, the founder of Arica, opened a school in Boulder. Samuel Avital, a student of Marcel Marceau, founded Le Centre du Silence Mime School in the foothills of the Rockies.

Journee met and had an audience with Swami Muktananda with only a few other people. Bhagavan Das had introduced Ram Das to Neem Karoli Baba and *Be Here Now* was published. The est Training was started by Werner Erhard. An amalgamation of Buddhist, Hindu, Greek, Jain, and Sufi traditions represented global cultures, deep heritages, and profound ways of viewing life. Transformation had arrived.

What was missing in Journee's academic pursuits was a sense of community and connectedness, internally and externally. She left the University of Colorado, heading for a quick stop in Marin, California, for a three-day retreat with Ram Dass and chanting by Krishna Das. Then on to Maui for a 30-day Vipassana retreat.

Reflecting back on this time in her life, Journee said, "My experiences were similar to taking a snow globe and shaking it, generating chaos. But at the same time there was an inexplicable peace, silence, and deep awareness of being home. This was the beginning of a long relationship with Neem Karoli Baba. I was rapidly becoming a Christian-Buddhist-Hindu."

Journee's family had a hard time relating to her newfound spirituality. Cultures and heritage clashed. "Coming home for the Christmas holiday," she said, "I was kidnapped by my parents and 'ushered' by force to a site in Vermont for a month-long deprogramming process."

Journee actually got along with the nuns and priests there. "We talked about God. I bided my time, knowing that after a month I would be free to go about my life."

When the time was up, Journee went to New York. There she touched base with a close friend and stayed with her in the Bronx. The small apartment was covered with pictures of spiritual beings and places. Journee participated in a Black Hat ceremony with His Holiness Karmapa, and met and had an audience with Kalu Rimpoche. Healing had begun. She had found her spiritual home.

SPIRITUALITY

Spirituality can be understood from multiple perspectives and practices worldwide. It is another element of our unique nature that makes us unlike anything else on earth.

Tracing its root word of origin back to the Latin, *spiritus*, spirit means soul, courage, vigor, breath. It can be the guideline of our lives and our values, what determines our psychological growth, and what drives personal transformation.

Spiritual wiring is part of our composition. Researchers have noted that there is something beyond the immediately tangible world in humans. Dr. Andrew Newberg has shown that a change occurs in the frontal lobes of our brains during focus and concentration. Long-term meditators (with at least 15 years of practice) have denser frontal lobes in comparison with those who don't meditate. When the frontal lobes are thicker there are health advantages (e.g., elevated memory). Levels of cortisol (a stress hormone) decrease when spirituality in some form is part of our lives.

Everyone wants their lives to have meaning. We all want to have value. We all want care and love to be part of our lives and help connect us to our world. And we all need to remember to exercise gratitude in our lives. As educators, these are basic tenets in our daily interactions with students.

SPIRITUALITY AND RELIGION

Spirituality is different from religion. Spirituality is our private connection to our selves where our souls can speak to us. Spirituality is often linked to a religious practice. Worship can be part of this. Prayer can be spoken or observed in silence. When our spirituality becomes linked to religion and we identify as Christians, or Buddhists, or Muslims, there are practices that we follow and these define us as part of that religious community. For some, religion is a large part of their identity and a religious community becomes part of their extended family.

Religion permeates society through our actions, our speech, our politics, our overall understanding of social responsibility, and our accountability to one another as human beings. Families, neighborhoods, even entire cities can be brought together or diminished by adherence to specific religious practices.

History has shown that religion can be a weapon of mass destruction. There have been numerous wars fought over religious expression. Every now and then I think that Jesus would be pulling his hair out if he saw how his words have been interpreted and put into action. He would probably welcome all the help he could get from the Buddha, Rama, Judah haNasi, Laozi, Parshva, Confucius, and Muhammad, to name a few!

But spirituality and religion don't need to limit our connections to one another. We can practice multiple religions without shunning our brothers and sisters. We can allow ourselves to be connected as one human family through acceptance, care, and love.

SPIRITUALITY IN STORYTELLING AND EDUCATION

Storytelling can be deeply spiritual when it reaches down into the very core of our being. We are the creators of our own stories, and we decide what to share with others. We know our limitations, our dark moments, that keep us from being who we truly are.

Yet we can be our own liberators. When we surround ourselves with loving, positive people and share our stories openly with them, we can find peace. We can free ourselves and then the world. Storytelling generates meaning in our lives and in the lives of others, even in the classroom.

Students are constantly exploring their identity, including their spiritual and religious understanding, in school settings. Identity is important in self-expression, in being safe and comfortable with others and ourselves. We can teach and support healthy identity development by knowing and using our own story and the stories of others.

In my teaching, students will frequently say that religion and spirituality are significant aspects of their identity. And yet they often hesitate to openly discuss their religious or spiritual views. Most of this student reluctance seems to stem from fear of judgment or having their views minimized. Also, everyone in my classroom understands that educators should not cross federal guidelines regulating religious expression in public schools.

The United States was founded on principles of religious liberty. The Pew Research Religion & Public Life Project Religious Landscape Survey identified eight main religious groups in the United States, with multiple associated affiliations. The United States ranked 68th for religious diversity among the 232 participating countries and territories. Although Christianity is the dominant religion (78% of the population), some sources report that there are more than 310 religions and denominations in the United States.

This diversity should be honored in our schools. Opportunities to explore religion and spirituality in school have been limited. However, assuming a foundation of civil discourse in our classes, we can explore religious and spiritual practices through history, literature, geography, philosophy, and music. Our students can further develop their personal identity and global perspective. They can learn to practice civil discourse, respect, and cooperation and ultimately continue the process of envisioning peace.

JOURNEE REVISITED

Education, spiritual practice, and family ultimately became the vehicle for Journee's healing. She started her own lineage with three biological and two step-children, making sure they understood the power of learning and the rich cultures of the world.

Armed with degrees, Journee explored the world and the beauty of education. Travels to Africa, India, Thailand, Nepal, Tibet, New Mexico, and Alaska have helped her understand who she is and her role in the world. Travel has revealed the value and power of education.

Education is central to Journee's work. As a teacher she has the possibility to touch lives, helping others to see the power, beauty, and privilege of an education. Her experiences in education have been vast. From teacher to school founder, she has embraced the gift of learning. As an instructor of teachers, Journee can light the passion and responsibility of teaching within her students. She works with them to understand the power of caring, the importance of knowing your students' stories, and the transformative nature of learning.

Ultimately, Journee's identity has become focused on wanting peace for others and herself. Her work is far from complete, and she sees each moment as fertile ground for greater spiritual integration.

CHAPTER 4

JOHN: IN OUR SCHOOLS

"The main aim of education should be a moral one,
that of nurturing the growth of competent, caring, loving,
and loveable persons."
- Nel Noddings

John: first row, far right

STANDING NEXT TO JOHN, I could feel small. He's 6' 4", with hands that easily cover a football. However, I don't. His smile is warm and vast, lighting up his face and those around him.

Born to Lorene and Edmund Shinsky on November 5, 1951, John's birthplace was a rough and tumble neighborhood in Lorain, Ohio. When John was 8 years old his father died of a heart attack. His mother thought it best to send John away from the tough neighborhood, so off he went to the Parmadale Orphanage.

I start all of my classes with the *CBS Sports Final Four Pre-Game Shinsky Orphanage Feature*. When John found out about this, he volunteered to come to as many of my classes as he can.

In talking about his background, John tells the students that he watched out the back window of the car as he was driven away. "It hit me right in the heart," he said. "I lost my father and the next thing that happens is I lose my family." He spent four years at the orphanage until his foster family welcomed him into their home.

John was introduced to sports by his foster family in high school and soon was recruited by numerous universities, including Ohio State, Notre Dame, and the University of Michigan, before he chose Michigan State University. A knee injury ultimately changed his path. "If it doesn't work out as expected, take another path," he thought. So he did.

John's philosophy is if one door is closed, there will be many more opened; you just have to find them, walk through, and take advantage of every opportunity available. The education field opened up to John. He started taking classes and soon found himself so far into education that it was the obvious path to follow.

For years, John had pondered how his mother could abandon him. "When I was no longer a ward of the state, I could go back and see my mom," he explained. "I couldn't imagine what kind of answer she could give that would satisfy me because I did not think there was a good answer to that question. But I just needed to know. When I walked into the house, I saw that there were some pictures on the wall of me playing football. I didn't think she'd kept up with me. And she said to me, 'I gave you up because I loved you more than I loved myself.'"

In 1983, John invited his mother to watch his doctoral graduation ceremony at Michigan State University. He bought her a new outfit and took her to have her hair done. On the following Monday his mother died of a brain aneurysm. He buried her in the same outfit.

At his mother's funeral a woman came up to him. Marie Cesare reintroduced herself as John's maternal grandmother. She informed him that his mother was her adopted child. John and his wife, Cindy, opened their home to Marie, where she lived out her life surrounded by their loving care.

"Marie taught me what unconditional love was," John said. "And she also taught me that ordinary people can do extraordinary things. You talk about unconditional love for somebody. That, to me, is a role model — she gave unselfish, unconditional love. That is why I have to give back."

After 27 years with the Lansing Public Schools as a teacher, administrator, and director of special education, he started an orphanage in Matamoros, Mexico. John does not stand on the sidelines of his life. Efforts to raise funds for the City of the Children of Matamoros, Mexico (Ciudad de los Niños Orphanage) continued as he battled a cancerous tumor in his neck quite close to the base of his skull.

"If you can survive it, it can become a strength," he said with a smile. This is the attitude that John teaches and leads from. "Demonstrate that you care. When you do things for other people, miracles happen."

Currently, there are 45 children in Ciudad de los Niños Orphanage, with plans to expand. John wants to empower young people with education, skills, and spirituality in a caring environment. He wants the children to strive to be leaders in their lives and in the lives of the people that they meet.

He left my class one day with the following advice to the students. "Ask yourself, 'What did you do today that really matters?' I got here because of other people like you. And remember, everyone has a story to share."

EDUCATION: CARING AT THE GLOBAL LEVEL

Nel Noddings' work has illuminated the importance of caring for others in education. She speaks and writes about the importance of remaining in connection. She focuses on our ability to listen and respond not only in our classrooms, but beyond those walls.

This ethic of care has the potential to extend throughout the world's families, communities, and societies. In times of tension there is a tendency to withdraw, but these are precisely the times when we must maintain connection and infuse conflict with care. Former United States Senator J. William Fulbright understood this and created the Fulbright Program — an international exchange program that builds long-term connections and shares our students, artists, educators, and scientists with nations around the world.

An important question must be answered by all educators. What do we want for all children of the human family beyond a basic ability to read, write, and do math? To empower students with the capacity to care? To learn how to treat one another honorably? To inspire hope and purpose? To help them develop the capacity to contribute to something beyond themselves?

If so, this is hard work. It requires self-exploration and knowing ourselves through our cultural identity, feelings, experiences, and individual heritage. This self-reflection can ultimately open up the larger world we live in.

CARING IN THE CLASSROOM

When I am teaching, I often assume that the children and young adults I have in my classrooms are from families with at least one parent. According to the U.S. Department of Health and Human Services, there are approximately 101,840 children in the United States waiting to be adopted, and the average age of these children is 7.7 years old. There are an estimated 153 million orphans in the world. American families have adopted approximately 179,719 children worldwide during the past 10 years. These facts are compounded by the number of foster children in the United States waiting to be adopted, exiting foster care, or "aging out" of the foster system. There are more than 402,378 children in foster care in the United States. Compare all of these statistics with the number of caring adults needed to change the life of a child: one.

The more I teach, the more I see that caring is the pivotal axis for success in education. At its best, caring is in the very nature of our profession — in our instructional style, lessons, classroom management, and ability to spark passion and hope beyond our classroom walls. And yet when asked, most educators don't say that care for their students is at the heart of their curriculum. Instead, measurable knowledge culminating in tests of achievement has become the core of many teachers' instructional process. This is ironic because most educators care deeply about their students and colleagues.

I believe care is expressed when we are responsive. To be responsive, we must listen to the stories of our students and be attentive to the needs they express. This is when the very essence of education can reveal itself — when a bond is formed between the educator and the student. We ultimately learn from one another in the fine dance of teaching.

A Learning Map for Caring in Education

As John's life has shown, our experiences as educators are going to be vastly different — as different as a university classroom in the Midwestern United States and the classroom in an orphanage in Mexico. These differences should be appreciated and celebrated, used to enhance our own and our students' lives, build connections, and create greater outreach. There also can be shared aims in those differences.

If I could create a map for learning that illustrates Nel Noddings' focus on care in education, it would contain many trails, and I would urge students to travel them all. My hope for not only my students, but every student near and far, is to reach out and follow as many trails as possible. I want them to learn how to build relationships; develop lifelong learning skills; belong to a community; and contribute to, share with, and appreciate others.

To help our students do this, we must lead by example. How can we teach about building relationships, contributing to communities, and appreciating others if we ourselves are incapable of doing so? Developing these aspects of ourselves as human beings significantly raises the bar of what we are capable of as educators, which ultimately changes the lives of our students and everyone they interact with. And once these skills are learned, they can never be unlearned. They will forever continue to foster care for our world, each other, and ourselves.

BUILD RELATIONSHIPS

Getting to know someone takes time. We rarely stop to ask each other about our life stories, and yet this is the most powerful way to build sustainable relationships.

Students need to learn how to do this — how to safely and sincerely share personal stories that can create connections. This must be taught; it isn't something they know how to do intuitively. We may come from different communities, but once we share our stories, our history can be validated and our understanding and empathy can grow.

DEVELOP LIFELONG LEARNING SKILLS

Education is continually happening within and far beyond the classroom walls. Every moment of our lives can become a learning moment. It's important that students develop this capacity to always be learning.

Within this process we need to help them foster a sense of confidence and competency. They need to develop their communication skills, understand problem-solving and coping skills, and identify their own personal assets and strengths. And they need to find their own voice for sharing their personal stories.

BELONG TO A COMMUNITY

Belonging to a community is important to all human beings. To belong is to develop sustainable partnerships and a common vision among people who have different perspectives. Students need to learn how to appreciate the value that diversity brings. They need to hear different voices and learn how to create access so those voices can belong. The ideal is to develop a sense of community that extends beyond "home" throughout all of creation.

CONTRIBUTE AND SHARE

Mutual care and shared responsibility connects people, providing them with opportunities to grow in their own lives and influence the lives of others. Students need to learn by example that we all have something to give to one another — that, no matter how young they are, they have something valuable to contribute to the world.

APPRECIATE OTHERS

Every day is a new day. Wake up with gratitude, and share a smile throughout the day. Students are drawn to learn from those who are positive, who understand how to rise above our differences, break down barriers, and forge new paths. They will learn to appreciate others when they see teachers working for and appreciating their students.

JOHN REVISITED

John's story is one of overcoming obstacles that could have derailed his life at any point in his childhood and teens. Hearing his story generates the kind of hope that can lead to action and change on a worldwide scale.

When we talked a second time, it was over a working lunch. Time is very valuable, but John will always make time to connect. I wanted to glean insight into his transition from pro football possibilities to becoming an educator. He started by reflecting on his childhood experiences at the orphanage.

Once, when John went back to visit Parmadale Orphanage, he realized how blessed he was to have his foster family. He told me about the tough gang leaders who were recruiting members out of the orphanage. John said that nobody really knew what happened there. He often felt trapped with no way out. Many of the students who were in the orphanage with John are now dead or imprisoned.

John never wanted to fail, and he didn't waste any opportunities. He said that he never really thought about the direction his studies were taking, but more about getting better at what he was doing. John wanted to collect all the tools of his field so he could be empowered to make a difference.

He started with a bachelor's degree in general and special education, which led to a master's degree in special education. A doctoral degree became a light at the end of a tunnel, and he completed his Ph.D. in educational leadership. The evolution of degrees became his commitment to stay the course and keep on the path.

Currently, the City of the Children (Ciudad de los Niños de Matamoros, A.C.) is flourishing, with many donations supporting the construction of additional dormitories and covering transportation and educational expenses. While this is wonderful, it's also alarming to think how many more children could benefit from someone like John.

One of John's many gifts is bringing people together. He is a leader and an educator with a gift for caring. His life and work have been enriched by the practice of caring. He refers to this as "penetrating the heart." He once said, "Doing things for people instead of having things may define a better path."

CHAPTER 5

HANNAH: A STRUGGLE FOR WELL-BEING

*"Every day is the journeying process.
There is no 'there' to arrive at, only the journey."*
- Hannah

BORN IN BRIDGEWATER, VERMONT, IN 1953, Hannah embraced the world, not just her life, with a profound sense of self at a young age. Hannah knew she was different. It was hard to be happy and she didn't understand the social "rules" for interacting with other people. But she couldn't talk with her parents about these differences. They were very conservative and she just knew they wouldn't get it. Hannah was alone, had almost no friends, and had no understanding why she was different.

When she was a teen, a new minister came to town and he was a "cool dude." He served as her counselor all the way through a miserable, depressed time in high school. She was bright and school was easy, so she threw herself into schoolwork as a way to cope and graduated with honors.

College proved to be her escape from home. For one year Hannah went to a small private college and then transferred to a larger liberal arts university, where she found some kinship in an alternative, experimental college.

"I was finally free," she said when we talked." But I was beginning to be even more overtly depressed than I'd been in high school, cycling in and out of bad times. But I somehow kept up the academics."

The backdrop to Hannah's story is one of turmoil. Politically, the United States was on fire with the feminist movement and Vietnam War protests, and she was on the front line of both. After experimenting with various street drugs, Hannah's drug of choice for depression became work. She quickly moved through her B.A. in 3-½ years. From then on, society highly rewarded her work ethic — in her words, her "addiction to being a workaholic."

A few years later, Hannah had completed an M.A. and had the start of an impressive resume. She then decided to move to another state to continue her career. After six years, in her late 30s, Hannah reflected on her success. She was very successful in her work and yet it was getting harder to maintain that level of success and control. Hannah knew she needed support and fortunately found a great counselor on the first try. They worked together successfully and the counselor got her through several serious depressive episodes.

Then one spring she began rapidly cycling between low-grade mania and deep depression. When her counselor saw the cycles occurring, she diagnosed Hannah with Type 2 bipolar disease. It turned out that genetically this diagnosis was present in the family. Her counselor referred Hannah to a psychiatrist, who confirmed the diagnosis and began to try a series of different drugs. Unfortunately, nothing worked.

"The day came when I sat in a chair for 12 hours without moving," Hannah explained. "If I could have killed myself without leaving a body behind for someone to clean up, I would have done it without a second thought."

Eventually Hannah reached for the phone and called her counselor. Then, summoning what little was left of her amazing strength, she drove herself to the local psychiatric ward. After a week, they found a medication combination that seemed to work.

During the next year her resilience, determination, and strength led her to move back to Vermont to start her own business and continue life. Once again, she quickly found a highly skilled practitioner — a new psychiatrist in town. Then suddenly, the drugs that had been helping turned on her.

"The drugs ended up not solving the brain disorder problem," she said. "They just helped me hang on to a miserable, exhausting life. So late that May I told my psychiatrist that if I wasn't noticeably better by July 4, I would commit suicide."

It happened that Hannah's psychiatrist had just met an individual who practiced acupuncture and had developed his own experimental treatment methodology, which did not fit the traditional model for either Western or Eastern medicine.

One year later, with their combined help, Hannah was finally weaned off all of her medications. She'd been told for years that bipolar is not curable. At age 47 Hannah became living proof that the disease could be conquered. Both her psychiatrist and her acupuncturist remarked that they had never seen such a strong will to live.

Hannah's approach to obstacles is to be persistent and creative. "Go over it, around it, or under it. Find whatever will work, even if it's unconventional."

Hannah has a strong faith that has nothing to do with religion or morality. "The Universe has always thrown the right people in my path at the right time who have helped to keep me going. Having shaken hands with the Grim Reaper at a young age has taught me about compassion at a level I otherwise wouldn't have known. And I understand that my friends are my family. I wouldn't have made it without my friends along the way."

I came away from our conversation convinced that Hannah *cares*. She can listen, she has learned what life has spoken to her, she understands illness, and now she is a healer through her work — which, by the way, is no longer an addiction.

NUMBERS

Hannah's story represents the struggles of many, most of whom are unseen in daily life. The importance of Hannah's individual story should not be lost in statistics. And yet the numbers tell an often unheard and unacknowledged story. As you read through the following statistics, think about your classrooms. If you have 30 students, how many of them might be suffering from some form of mental illness?

The National Alliance on Mental Illness has published the following data for the United States:

* 20% of youth ages 13-18, and 13% of those ages 8-15, experience severe mental disorders in a given year.
* 70% of youth in juvenile justice systems have at least one mental health condition; at least 20% live with a severe mental illness.
* 60% of adults (and almost one-half of youth ages 8-15) with a mental illness received no mental health services in the previous year.
* One-half of all chronic mental illness begins by the age of 14, and three-quarters by age 24.
* 50% of students with a mental health condition age 14 and older who are served by special education drop out of school — the highest dropout rate of any disability group.

And finally, Find Youth Info breaks this down further. Nearly half of United States adolescents meet criteria for mental health disorders: 14.3% with mood disorders, 31.9% with anxiety disorders, 19.6% with behavior disorders, and 11.4% with substance use disorders.

BEYOND THE NUMBERS

The 2013 Substance Abuse and Mental Health Services Administration (SAMHSA) report stated that 19.2% of the United States' adult population has mental health concerns, approximately one in five adults. But these people are more than contributors to a statistic. The raw numbers often blind us to the reality that these are real individuals who are suffering every day with devastating illnesses.

How many brilliant people have we confined, shunned, drugged, or shut down because they didn't fit the educational mold? Genius is a term loosely used and yet some of the world's most creative people struggled with mental health concerns: Michelangelo, Abraham Lincoln, Charles Dickens, Virginia Woolf, Marie Sklodwska-Curie, Joan of Arc, Henry Ford, and Winston Churchill. Clearly, mental well-being concerns all of humanity.

MENTAL HEALTH IN SCHOOL

The Center for Disease Control describes mental health in childhood as the "achievement of developmental and emotional milestones, healthy social development, and effective coping skills, such that mentally healthy children have a positive quality of life and can function well at home, in school and in their communities."

Under this definition, Hannah didn't come anywhere close to mental health. She knew she was "different" from an early age, but she couldn't reach out within her family or school because she didn't feel safe. Somehow, she understood intuitively as a child that if she said anything, she would create an even greater hell than she was already experiencing. And as a teenager and young adult, she clearly understood the stigma associated with the social norms of mental health. It wasn't until the "cool dude" minister came to town that she was able to share her story with anyone and start down a long road toward healing.

Rosalyn Carter has stated that the stigma around mental health must change. We all have bodies, hearts, and minds. We openly discuss our physical health, and yet our mental and emotional well-being remain shrouded, cloaked in the very shadow that they need to emerge from.

One indication of the value placed on mental health is that most of our schools offer no curriculum or instruction on mental health. Student concerns that manifest in substance abuse, eating disorders, bullying, and gang affiliation are often addressed on the surface and without understanding the depth of the issue. What is managed temporarily might arise again in another manifestation. We are often applying a bandage without treating the wound.

The current ratio of students to school counselors is 471:1. The recommended ratio is 250:1. This is far too high to have a daily influence on the needs of our students. But schools are often wary of addressing mental health. Some school personnel state that schools are there just to educate. Others counter that if students aren't succeeding, there is an overlap between a school's mission and students' mental well-being.

Addressing obstacles to learning and teaching can become a context for pursuing the needed scope of psychosocial and mental health services. This would require teachers, staff, and administrators to re-envision how services could be provided — blending community resources and rethinking the current health profession/social work/criminal justice approach to educating our students and staying healthy.

Hannah Revisited

The importance of transformative relationships and intentional caring punctuates Hannah's story. Person after person — friends and practitioners — came into her life at precisely the time they were most needed.

But Hannah's story left me pondering about her early years. Where were the school counselors when she was a child? Did any of her teachers pick up on anything during all those years? Or can smart students like Hannah get so good at passing through a system that they become invisible, appearing to be highly successful but suffering deeply?

Several months after our original conversation, Hannah and I talked again. She told me that she never expected to live this long, so she tries to remember that every day is a gift and to not take anything for granted.

Hannah is approaching retirement age, and she told me that the physical process of aging has been like a "slap across the face." She sees her life journey as a spiral — dealing now in another form with some of the lessons she first learned when she was struggling with mental illness. But no matter what happens to her in the future, Hannah believes her story will always be a testimony to the caring of others, persistence, and hope.

Envisioning Peace

CHAPTER 6

ISAIAH: THE COURAGE TO BEGIN AGAIN

"Nothing is impossible, the word itself says 'I'm possible'!"
- Audrey Hepburn

Peering over Kim's shoulder, I glimpsed a photo of a young man with beautiful skin tone, eyes closed, with a slight smile on his face. His arms were wrapped around a woman, her blonde hair attractively done in an updo. She was formally dressed in a stunning purple gown that cascaded in ruffles to the floor. A wheelchair was in the foreground. This is how I first "met" Isaiah.

Kim is our office coordinator. She runs a tight ship in an academic circle of practitioners whose forgetfulness runs from office keys to appointments. The walls of her cubicle are adorned with family photos. She told me that this was a picture from her daughter's wedding. Isaiah is her son-in-law. Isaiah was holding up his birth mother, and the two were dancing.

When I saw it, I immediately knew I wanted to be able to use the photo in my class and I wanted to meet this young man. As someone who teaches social and cultural diversity, this one photo encompassed many of the perspectives we cover: race, gender, and disability. It also went beyond what is typically taught, addressing love, compassion, upbringing, and life's experiences. I eventually discovered that Isaiah's story represented a journey of diversity and the power of caring.

On the day we actually met, Isaiah walked into the restaurant, which he had picked, and began settling into his chair as I went up and introduced myself. Dressed in a freshly pressed orange dress shirt with a black vest, he let me know that he had "quickly gone home and showered and changed." His gentle ease, infectious smile, firm handshake, and sparkling green eyes helped me relax into this rural restaurant, where initially I had felt self-conscious.

Isaiah was born in Allegan, Michigan, on August 17, 1985. He dove into our conversation.

"Who the hell am I? I am a good guy. I care about people. I am very smart and intelligent. But I crashed at 19 after I'd started molding a tough image of myself at 8 or 9 years old. My aunt and uncles were all Hell's Angels. My mom got kicked out of the house at 16, and then she got pregnant. My father was into drugs and crack and a pimp on the side and all this other stuff, and he beat her a lot.

"Then when I was born, things got even worse. No one in my family wanted anything to do with me. My father was duct-taping me to the crib and duct-taping the bottle to my face and locking me in the bedroom. My mom was so scared she would piss on herself. He took a boot, like a cowboy dance boot with a heel, and smashed her in the head with it.

"I was in the bathtub one night. She had a seizure while she was giving me a bath and fell in the water. I was crying. She was underwater having a seizure. I was just a kid, so I thought, 'If I ignore this it will just go away, and it won't happen.'"

After his birth mother's seizure, Isaiah's aunt and family stepped in to take over his care. He went to a private school in Grandville, Michigan, that he called "all White."

Isaiah continued his story. "I tried to fit in with that school, but it gave me a huge identity crisis. I didn't fit in around Black people, and I didn't fit in around White people. Geez oh Pete. What do you do? Stuff started coming back up. I had temper tantrums. I slammed my head against the wall. I couldn't figure out why I was angry.

"Everybody, counselors, said it was not right, not okay to act how you are acting. I had to pretend to be normal in society or whatever."

Isaiah was held back in 7th grade. He was drawn to the young boys who had the girls and were on the football team. When he was 14 he asked a student how he did it, how he became the popular one. The student laughed at him and Isaiah swore he would never ask again. "I am going to keep on image molding until I get it right," he vowed to himself.

He eventually dropped out of high school. Soon parties, drugs, alcohol, and sex began. One night after partying, Isaiah offered to drop off a young woman who needed a ride home. Isaiah was dating the woman who would eventually become his wife. He did not want to engage in sexual activities with the young woman he was driving home.

The young woman said she was going to be sick, so Isaiah pulled over. They were on a very populated road with streetlights and businesses. She started kissing Isaiah and then a police officer pulled behind them. She got upset and Isaiah assured her that the most she would get would be an MIP and to relax. The young woman jumped out of the car crying and said he was having sex with her.

Isaiah ended up serving six years for a crime he did not commit. "What I figured out in prison was that I was trying to get happiness from gratification, but you will never get it like that no matter how hard you try. Plus, how many people can say they were around murderers and robbers and people who would kill you in your sleep? At work now I can talk with the president of the company and I can talk just the same as I did with them.

So I am grateful for my experience there." To me, this truly demonstrated Isaiah's authentic connection with people and his ability to comfortably communicate with everyone.

Isaiah told me he still ponders how unconditional love has transformed his life. After he got out of prison, he moved into his own home with his wife and young son. He had been working long hours and had just interviewed for a promotion in management when we had our conversation. Every day he has challenges to stay on track. But he knows he is loved, his own love is overwhelming, and his laugh is irresistible.

I hugged Isaiah when I left and then said goodbye. After leaving the bathroom I jumped into my car, conscious that someone was across the parking lot. As I pulled out Isaiah flashed his lights, having waited until I was safely on my way.

"You can choose to be happy," I remember him saying. "Your level of caring, that is the most important thing. Once that is gone, it is hard to get back."

Coming in to work the next Monday morning Kim looked up and smiled at me. "So Isaiah says you are pretty cool." I shared with her how grateful Isaiah is to be with his wife and son and to be part of Kim's family. "He still is surprised by our unconditional love," she said.

THE PRISON/INDUSTRY COMPLEX

The United States has the highest incarceration rate in the world. With approximately 5% of the world's population, the United States has nearly 25% of the world's prisoners. Through no fault of his own, Isaiah became part of a prison/industry complex that incarcerates more of its youth than any other country.

Corrections is one of the fastest growing industries in the United States. The average cost of juvenile incarceration is $373 per day or $136,145 a year. That is roughly 10 times the cost of the average K-12 public education.

In 2005, Federal Prison Industries sold $750 million worth of items to the federal government. According to Pelaez, a leading author on prison reform, at least 37 states have legalized prison labor for private corporations that base their businesses inside state prisons. The list of such companies includes AT&T, Boeing, Compaq, Dell, Hewlett-Packard, Honeywell, IBM, Macy's, Microsoft, Motorola, Nordstrom's, Pierre Cardin, Revlon, Target Stores, Texas Instrument, TWA, and many more.

The largest private detention company, the Corrections Corporation of America, reported $1.7 billion dollars in total revenue in 2011. That same year the Geo Group, the second largest private detention company, reported $1.6 billion in total revenue. The average prisoner earns 25 cents per hour for their labor.

INCARCERATION BY RACE

The Sentencing Project states that 60% of people in prison are racial or ethnic minorities. In 2013, by the age of 18, 30% of Black males, 26% of Hispanic males, and 22% of White males had been arrested. By the age of 23, 49% of Black males, 44% of Hispanic males, and 38% of White males had been arrested. The Sentencing Project goes on to state that the lifetime possibility of imprisonment for Black males is 1 in 3, Latino males is 1 in 6, and White males is 1 in 17. Black youth make up 16% of the total population of the United States, but account for 28% of juvenile arrests.

How Did We Get Here?

VIOLENCE

Approximately six in 10 United States youth have been exposed to violence within the past year. This includes seeing a violent act, being assaulted with a weapon, being a victim of sexual assault, experiencing child maltreatment, or suffering violence while dating. Of that number, one in 10 was injured. In 2008, there were 772,000 reported child victims of maltreatment.

Isaiah experienced so much violence during his childhood that the odds of him becoming a victim were disproportionately high.

SCHOOL TO PRISON PIPELINE

The phrase "school to prison pipeline" is used to describe the pattern of thrusting students out of school and into the criminal justice system. The students who are excluded are often those already struggling and disadvantaged in their learning.

African American students like Isaiah are 3.5 times more likely than White students to be suspended or expelled. African American students make up approximately 18% of the student population, but are 46% of those suspended. Almost 8.6% of school-age children have disabilities, but they account for 32% of the population in juvenile detention centers. About one in four African American children with disabilities have been suspended at least once compared to one in 11 White children.

Policies and practices have created a system that is difficult to escape: police in the schools, drug dogs, searches of students and lockers, zero-tolerance policies, suspensions and expulsions, high-stakes testing, and a persistent covert institutional culture of racism.

We are all responsible for how we got here. This isn't a blame game. As educators we are all accountable and we must work to change the systems children are growing up in. Our students' lives depend on it. It's imperative that we begin a national discussion on how to save our children. That discussion needs to connect with education, social work, the criminal justice system, and the health care profession — anywhere professionals are being taught to care for children and families.

ISAIAH REVISITED

Within the first few minutes, Isaiah shared his story with me with incredible depth and openness. He knew I was an educator and that I valued his story. What he didn't realize was the effect his life story would have on my students and me. Protecting his identity, I shared part of his narrative in my undergraduate and graduate classes. I asked them, "As a teacher, how would you reach him?" I'm now working with the nursing, social work, education, and criminal justice departments in my university to re-envision how we educate our students to be more effective in promoting change with the people they serve.

Isaiah has stayed in touch. We communicate around major events in his life: a new baby, a job promotion, going back to school for a B.S. in engineering. While I would never want anyone to walk the harshness of his path, I do hold out hope that those who are living similar stories can find that unconditional love he did — a love that lifts us beyond our small worlds.

Envisioning Peace

ON THE STREETS

*"Learning is not something that you can turn on or off,
rather it is a fluid and ever-changing concept
that everyone utilizes."*
- Abby Lyons

THE FIVE NARRATIVES IN THIS book show how people worked through their suffering and transformed their lives through the power of care, compassion, and hard work. These individuals took control of their own journeys and went beyond the personal anguish that kept them bound on what seemed to be a predestined path. They actively made decisions that led them to a greater understanding of themselves and, as a result, they re-identified who they were on the path of their lives.

Where were the educators in Isaiah's and Hannah's lives? Did no one within the educational system notice the turmoil that these individuals were going through? Was no one able to make a connection with these young people? What powerful leaders John, Cindy, and Dorie are to practice unconditional love in the midst of relational turmoil and identity building. Do we have what it takes to do work like this? Is Journee's path toward spiritual exploration and religious broadmindedness one that can create acceptance and a more peaceful world?

Our lives have both profound diversity and intimate connectedness. Life stories like these convince me that caring is the thread that can run through and unite the various types of work involved with peace education. The principles and practices of caring vary as much as people do. However, no matter how varied we are, we all need care and connection.

A Call to Action

The power of narratives can change lives and lead us into a more compassionate version of ourselves. Narratives can create possibilities for a change in attitudes; we can become kinder to ourselves and, therefore, to others. The power of storytelling can shape consciousness in our lives. Stories go beyond the individual and reach into the fabric of our very being. Personal transformation becomes possible.

So now what? Moving into action is important. Daily we encounter numerous people — physically, on the phone, via e-mail and text. Life revolves around interactions and communication. We can learn so much from one another. Everyone has their own story, and our stories intersect with each other. Sometimes we collide; at other times we gently flow into one another's story. Within those moments, however brief they might be, we have the power to be present with one another.

Being present can mean making an active choice to listen, to empathize, to validate, and to care. Being present enables us to connect, to step beyond ourselves, and to allow our students' individual stories to enter into education. Gaining even a little information about someone — students or anyone else — can totally change our attitudes and how we view the situation, thus changing our stories and allowing the possibility for peace.

Guides for the Path

There are some universal guides for this type of action. I have patterned the guides described here after the Buddha's Noble Eightfold Path, although they don't have to be used toward religious merit. Instead, they can be seen as trail markers toward freedom, happiness, and peace through wisdom, ethical conduct, and intellectual development. These guides are not mutually exclusive, and yet they need to be individually developed and nurtured.

The Noble Eightfold Path addresses three important aspects necessary for a successful life: *wisdom, mental discipline,* and *ethical conduct.* Each has its own steps. Wisdom consists of proper view or understanding and right thought or intention. Mental discipline necessitates effort and concentration. Ethical conduct requires appropriate speech and action.

WISDOM

An educator's attunement with his/her self directly connects with instruction, relationships, the educational environment, and the well-being of all involved in the process of teaching and learning. Right view or understanding, coupled with our intentions and thoughts, generates the wisdom to accurately perceive ourselves and others. We are products of our experiences, and we bring who we are into all we do. It is of vital importance to know our students and ourselves. This knowledge incorporates a fine balance of intellectual grasp, emotional and mental well-being, physical response, and spiritual understanding.

Proper View/Understanding: We need to understand the situations we find ourselves in. There are two forms of this understanding: the fundamental understanding that stems from knowledge or intellectually comprehending something, and wisdom, which comes from a deeper appreciation of reality.

For example, a student walked into my classroom one day wearing all black with chains draping from his belt. Blaze was a new student. My mind immediately leapt to preconceived notions regarding clothing and names. As it turned out, Blaze was one of the most thoughtful students I had that year.

A basic understanding of leadership in teaching and learning requires that we see things as they really are. Our views often form our thoughts and actions. It is imperative to think things through clearly, with informed knowledge and intuitive insight, and to be open and allow time for this process to occur. Every action we take brings about a result. When we are motivated by compassion, the results are positive.

Right Intention/Thought: Right intention and thought require a commitment to uphold ethical and mental development. Present intentions, conscious or subconscious, shape and select what we actually experience in the moment. The Buddha listed three types of intentions:

- The intention of renunciation, to resist the tug of desire
- The intention of good will, to resist feelings of anger and loathing
- The intention of harmlessness, to not think or act aggressively or cruelly and to develop compassion

These present intentions add to the range of raw material from which we will select and shape experiences in the future. Past actions provide the raw material for our present experience. What actions now will lead to sustainable well-being and happiness for all? Happiness comes from our own actions, and we need wisdom or discernment to guide our actions.

Our ethical code as educators commands us to teach each and every student who comes into our schools. We strive to help our students do and be the best they can possibly master. Our challenge is to continually uphold our professional intentions for our students' success and well-being.

MENTAL DISCIPLINE

The mental discipline required to be a successful educator requires a fine balance in recognizing and responding to the thoughts and feelings of our students and ourselves. It requires an amazing amount of patience and the ability to be present without preconceived notions. That presence will initiate the capacity to identify and engage in situations appropriately. Gentle kindness, determination, and discipline are the powers inherent in sustainable effort, healthy mindfulness, and correct concentration.

Sustainable Effort: Every day we are called upon to make effort. Effort is often the root of all achievement, and it must be sustainable to help us go through our daily lives. We are not Samantha on the popular 1960s TV show *Bewitched*, where all she had to do was wiggle her nose and the work was done. Perseverance is important in our work. The effort we make also must be balanced. It requires a skillful cultivation of loving kindness, generosity, and wisdom. When we are in balance and we persevere in our work as educators, the effort we make in teaching flows naturally.

Healthy Mindfulness: The daily decisions and choices we make are often tenuous; we're tempted to choose a "short cut" that could result in a longer route. Healthy mindfulness means being aware. Being aware of what is happening in the moments of the teaching life of educators is the ultimate goal. No seizing, which is greed. No rebuking, which is hatred. No neglecting, which is delusion. Just observing with assurance, equilibrium, and steadiness.

When this happens, the day becomes a dance with poise and balance. Our thoughts do not control us; instead, we control our thoughts. We are alert and aware and not lost in worry, daydreams, anticipation, or mental indulgences. There is no longer a need to judge or filter our lives through subjective opinions. We are present in our own lives, aware of what we are supposed to be doing, seeing things as they really are — the true nature of the events in our lives. I am fond of telling my students to be present with one another. Their worries, work, and future endeavours will be at the door when and if they choose to pick them up after class.

Correct Concentration: The ability to stay focused — to concentrate correctly — is about the ability to stay centered, to maintain one-point-edness, and to not get lost or distracted in the details of our lives or in the vastness of our stories and our students' stories. When we practice staying in the moment and being present in our lives, it gets easier over time. It's like training for a marathon; the more time and effort you put in, the greater the results. Being present becomes a lifestyle.

Ethical Conduct

The guides of wisdom and mental discipline lead us to additional trail markers on this path for envisioning peace. They are *appropriate speech, respectable action,* and *proper livelihood.*

Appropriate Speech: The Dalai Lama has a simple exercise that illustrates right/appropriate speech. See how far you can go in a day without saying anything about someone who is not in your presence. In other words, you cannot talk about anyone else unless you are with them — a simple enough action, yet very difficult to do.

Right speech is not saying anything that hurts others: no lies, slander, ill will, or gossip. This means speaking only in a manner that could generate peace and harmony through the use of truthful and supportive language. This approach could make our relationships more peaceful, easier to navigate, and less complicated. Appropriate speech lends itself to being truthful and supportive with ourselves and others.

Respectable Action: This means working for the good of others. The aim is to promote moral, honorable, and peaceful behavior. We remain intentional and tactful despite our current circumstances or preconceived notions. Our actions are purposeful, manifesting generosity, virtue, and universal goodwill.

Acts of merit show the value and importance of our own actions. We have the ability to choose how we act. When we interact with people and bring an attitude of good will, the experience of the process is different than if we approach the situation with hostility.

Respectable action (i.e., working for the good of others) looks very different for each individual. Our actions have consequences, sometimes unintended. Isaiah acted and his actions eventually led him to prison. But he told me that, upon reflection, prison saved his life. If he hadn't been imprisoned, he might be dead. In despair, Hannah took a highly unconventional, risky path to healing that could have led to her death. But in the end she saved her own life.

The results of meritorious action can be so satisfying that they may interfere with our desire to do further work. But we cannot stop and rest on the virtue of our past actions. As educators, we are called upon daily to display compassion and good will in our work.

Proper Livelihood: This means to respect life and engage in a profession that promotes harmony for the individual and for society. S.N. Goenka says, "If the intention is to play a useful role in society in order to support oneself and to help others, then the work one does is right livelihood."

This implies that, as we do our individual work, we also depend on one another for support. Without moral, ethical, and personal support, being an educator is extraordinarily difficult. We must lead by example. We teach our students not only through our words, but through our actions. We, as educators, cannot uphold the foundations of education while acting as solitary pillars. It is imperative that we move cohesively as a group to uphold and strengthen the framework of education — to assure that students see how our right livelihood plays a useful role in society.

BRINGING IT ALL TOGETHER

All of these guides depend on one another. They are linked together to help foster growth and a peaceful life. René Daumal's *Mount Analogue* is a perfect analogy for understanding how these guides interact with one another in the stories of our lives. When climbing a mountain there are certain skillful actions that must be sustained: maintain an awareness of the path to the top of the mountain ... keep your eyes on the goal ... remember to look in front of you as you climb ... be aware of your footing ... take one step at a time. And remember to breathe.

In all of the narratives in this book, each individual cultivated a healthy sense of self, understanding their relationship to the world and combining that with a deepening appreciation and awareness of their own nature. They became aware of their own suffering and the suffering of those around them. They each understood that altering or transforming their actions could change suffering and that their paths were within their own power to change. They learned through experience where life's opportunities were.

We, too, have our own stories. We have our own opportunities.

"It is necessary to love peace and sacrifice for it."
- Martin Luther King, Jr.

SIMPLE GUIDE

I ENCOURAGE YOU TO TAKE a moment to pause and watch your breath as you breathe in and then exhale — a very deliberate moment where your thoughts become clouds and drift in and then out. Not thinking and not, not thinking. Just being. Watch the tension in your body as it speaks to you of the long time you've spent sitting in a chair or being on your feet. Then let your thoughts and tension sail out with your breath.

As educators, there are steps that can be practiced to envision peace in our daily work:

* Make a deliberate decision to care for yourself and your students.
* Engage with your students; listen sagaciously to what they have to say in their words *and* actions.
* Maintain a strong awareness of your thoughts and feelings as you go through your day. Stop and breathe. Get out into the fresh air, if only for a moment. Empathize with your students, but resist the fleeting or enabling compassion that gives them the easy way out.
* Display a teachable spirit. Unpack your own patterns and routines, and jump the wagon wheel ruts of your life.
* Act with integrity. Speak with thoughtfulness. Be gentle with yourself and others. Forgive. Learn. Move on.

Self-discipline and compassion are vital for our bodies, minds, and hearts to sustain the noble profession of education.

REFERENCES & RESOURCES

American School Counselor Association. *Student to-school-counselor ratio 2010-2011*. Retrieved from: http://www.schoolcounselor.org/asca/media/asca/home/Ratios10-11.pdf

Amura, C. (2013). Fact sheet: *How bad is the school-to-prison pipeline?* Retrieved from: http://www.pbs.org/wnet/tavissmiley/tsr/education-under-arrest/school-to-prison-pipeline-fact-sheet/

Bhikkhu, T. (2013). *Discernment: The Buddha's strategies for happiness.* Retrieved from: http://www.dhammatalks.org/Archive/Writings/Discernment_v130716.pdf

Bonczar, T. (2003). *Prevalence of Imprisonment in the U.S. Population, 1974-2001.* Washington, D.C.: Bureau of Justice Statistics.

Centers for Disease Control and Prevention. *Children's Mental Health.* (2014). Retrieved from: http://www.cdc.gov/ncbddd/childdevelopment/mentalhealth.html

Daumal, R. (1992). *Mount Analogue: A novel of symbolically authentic non-Euclidean adventures in mountain climbing.* Boston: Shambala.

Elias, M. (2013). *School to prison pipeline: Policies and practices that favor incarceration over education do us all a grave injustice.* Teaching Tolerance. Retrieved from: http://www.tolerance.org/sites/default/files/general/School-to-Prison.pdf

Find Youth Info. (2013). *Prevalence of mental health disorders among youth.* Retrieved from: http://www.findyouthinfo.gov/img/ymh_infographic.png

Forty to None 2015. *People do not choose to be homeless-particularly young people.* Retrieved from: http://fortytonone.org/get-informed/learn-about the-issue/overview/

GLSEN National School Climate Survey. (2014). Retrieved from: http://glsen.org/article/glsen-releases-new-national-school-climate-survey

Goenka, S.N., edited by Hart, W. (1987). *The art of living: Vipassana Meditation as taught by S.N. Goenka.* Onalaska, WA: Vipassana Research Publications.

Henrichson, C. & Delaney, R. (2012). *The price of prisons: What incarceration costs taxpayers.* VERA Institute of Justice: Center on Sentencing and Corrections.

Holland, J. (December 16, 2013). *Land of the free? US has 25 percent of the world's prisoners.* Retrieved from: http://billmoyers.com/2013/12/16/land-of-the-free-us-has-5-of-the-worlds-population-and-25-of-its-prisoners/

Holman, B. & Ziedenberg, J. (2006). *The dangers of detention: The impact of incarcerating youth in detention and other secure facilities.* A Justice Policy Institute Report.

Kovensky, J. (2014). *It's time to pay prisoners the minimum wage.* Retrieved from: http://www.newrepublic.com/article/119083/prison-labor-equal-rights-wages-incarcerated-help-economy

Lee, S. (2012). *By the numbers: The U.S.'s Growing for profit detention industry.* Retrieved from: http://www.propublica.org/article/by-the-numbers-the-u.s.s-growing-for-profit-detention-industry

Losen, D. (2012). *Opportunities suspended: The disparate impact of disciplinary exclusion from school.* The Center for Civil Rights Remedies at The Civil Rights Project.

McCormack, S. (2014). *Nearly half of black males, 40 percent of white males are arrested by age 23: Study.* huffingtonpost.com.

National Alliance on Mental Illness. (2013). *Mental Illness Facts and Numbers.* Retrieved from: http://www.nami.org/factsheets/mentalillness_factsheet.pdf

National Center for Educational Statistics. (2012). *Public elementary and secondary school student enrollment and staff counts from the common core of data: School year 2010-2011.* Retrieved from: http://nces.edgov/pubs2012/2012327.pdf

National Council on Crime and Delinquency. (2007). *And justice for some: differential treatment of youth of color in the Justice System.*

National Kids Count Report. (2014). *Per-pupil educational expenditures adjusted for regional cost differences.* Retrieved from: http://www.datacenter.kidscount.org/data/tables/5199-per-pupil-educational-expenditures-adjusted-for-regional-cost-di#detailed/1/any/false/867,133,38,35,18/any/11678

National Research Council & Institute of Medicine. (2009). *Preventing mental, emotional, and behavioral disorders among young people: Progress and possibilities.* Committee on the Prevention of Mental Disorders and Substance Abuse among Children, Youth, and Young Adults: Research Advances and Promising Interventions. O'Connell, M.E., Boat, T., & Warner, K.E. (Eds.) Board on Children, Youth, and Families, Division of Behavioral and Social Sciences and Education. Washington, DC: National Academies Press.

Newberg, A. & Waldman, M. (2009). *How God changes your brain.* NY: Random House.

Pelaez, V. (2014). *The prison industry in the United States: Big business or a new form of slavery?* Retrieved from: http://www.globalresearch.ca/the-prison-industry-in-the-united-states-big-business-or-a-new-form-of-slavery/8289

Pew Research Religion and Public Life Project. (2015). *Religious landscape survey.* Retrieved from: http://religions.pewforum.org/reports

ProCon.org. (2008). *Under God in the pledge: Pros and cons.* Retrieved from: http://undergod.procon.org/view.resource.php?resourceID=000068

Ray, N. (2006). *Lesbian, bisexual, transgender youth: An epidemic of homelessness.* National Gay and Lesbian Task Force Policy Institute and the National Coalition for the Homeless.

The Sentencing Project. (2013). *Report of The Sentencing Project to the United Nations Human Rights Committee regarding racial disparities in the United States Criminal Justice System.* Retrieved from: http://sentencingproject.org/doc/publications/rd_ICCPR%20Race%20and%20Justice%20Shadow%20Report.pdf

Tokuhama-Espinosa, T. (2011). *A brief history of the science of learning: Part 1 (3500 B.C.E.-1970 C.E.)* Retrieved from: http://education.jhu.edu/PD/newhorizons/Journals/Winter2011/Tokuhama4

UNICOR (Federal Prisons Industries). (2008). *Factories with fences: 75 years of changing lives.* Retrieved from: https://www.unicor.gov/information/publications/pdfs/corporate/CATMC1101_C.pdf

U.S. Department of Health and Human Services. (2012). *Results from the 2012 national survey on drug use and health.* Retrieved from: http://www.samhsa.gov/data/NSDUH/2012SummNatFindDetTables/NationalFindings/NSDUHresults2012.htm

U.S. Department of Health and Human Services. (2010). *Child maltreatment 2008.* Retrieved from: http://www.acf.hhs.gov/programs/cb/pubs/cm08/cm08.pdf

U.S. Department of Health and Human Services. (2009). *Results from the 2008 national survey on drug use and health: National findings.* Retrieved from: http://oas.samhsa.gov/nsduh/2k8nsduh/2k8Results.cfm

Wagner, P. (2003). *Prison policy initiative.* Retrieved from: http://www.prisonpolicy.org/prisonindex/prisonlabor.html

Envisioning Peace

ABOUT THE AUTHOR

Susan F. Carson is a professor of education in the College of Education at Grand Valley State University in Grand Rapids, Michigan. Dr. Carson's scholarship and research focuses include the implementation of peace education in urban K-12 schools, social justice and peace education with a multicultural emphasis, and peace and justice studies in international education. She developed a model program with Kent School Services Network (a social service network with 21 organizations and six school districts), teaching undergraduate students at identified schools serving homeless youth.

Dr. Carson's 2010 Fulbright Award to research "Principles and Practices of Caring Communities: Women's Participation in the Public Spheres of Education in Contemporary India" demonstrated her effectiveness as a cross-cultural educator and negotiator. Her international research in peace education has included work with the University of Education, Pädagogische Hochschule Schwäbisch Gmünd, Germany; Lucknow University, Lucknow, India; the University of Cape Coast, Ghana; the Northern Council for Integrated Education in Belfast; and the Consultores Associados in Uberaba, Brazil.